Bilingual Edition

READING POWER

Edición Bilingüe

Record-Breaking Animals

The Giraffe

World's Tallest Animal

La jirafa

El animal más alto del mundo

Joy Paige

The Rosen Publishing Group's
PowerKids Press™ & Buenas Letras™
New York

Published in 2003 by The Rosen Publishing Group, Inc.
29 East 21st Street, New York, NY 10010
Copyright © 2003 by The Rosen Publishing Group, Inc.

First Bilingual Edition 2003
First Edition in English 2002

Book Design: Sam Jordan
Photo Credits: Cover © Artville; pp. 5, 7, 12–13, 15, 17, 19, 21 © Indexstock; pp. 9, 11 © Animals Animals

Paige, Joy
The Giraffe: World's tallest animal/La jirafa: El animal más alto del mundo/Joy Paige ; traducción al español: Spanish Educational Publishing
p. cm. — (Record-Breaking Animals)
Includes bibliographical references and index.
ISBN 0-8239-6895-2 (lib. bdg.)
1. Giraffe—Juvenile literature. [1. Giraffe. 2. Spanish Language Materials—Bilingual.] I. Title.

Printed in The United States of America

Contents _____

_____ Contenido

Giraffes are tall animals. They live in Africa.

Las jirafas son muy altas.
Viven en África.

Africa

África

5

Giraffes are taller than some trees.

Las jirafas son más altas
que algunos árboles.

Giraffes are 6 feet (1.8m) tall at birth. They grow about an inch each day. Giraffes can grow to be 18 feet (5.4m) tall.

Las jirafas miden 6 pies (1.8m) de altura cuando nacen. Crecen una pulgada por día. Las jirafas pueden medir 18 pies (5.4m) de altura.

Giraffes have very long necks. Their long necks help them get food. Giraffes eat the leaves from the tall trees.

Las jirafas tienen
el cuello muy largo.
Con su cuello largo
alcanzan la comida.
Las jirafas comen las hojas
de los árboles altos.

Giraffes also have long tongues. Their tongues are 18 inches (45.7cm) long! Their tongues help them rip the leaves from the trees.

Las jirafas también tienen
la lengua muy larga.
¡Mide 18 pulgadas (45.7cm)!
Las jirafas arrancan las hojas
de los árboles con la lengua.

It is hard for giraffes to reach
water. They must spread their
legs to drink.

A las jirafas les cuesta
alcanzar el agua.
Tienen que separar las patas
para beber agua.

15

Giraffes have long legs. Their long legs help them run fast. Giraffes can run up to 35 miles (56km) an hour.

———————————————

Las jirafas tienen patas largas. Con ellas corren muy rápido. Las jirafas pueden correr a 35 millas (56km) por hora.

Giraffes also have very good eyes. They can see for miles. They can smell and hear well, too.

Las jirafas tienen buena vista. Pueden ver a muchas millas. También tienen buen olfato y buen oído.

Giraffes are taller than any other animal. They are more than 10 feet (3m) taller than zebras. They are the tallest of all animals.

Las jirafas son los animales más altos del mundo.
Miden más de 10 pies (3m) más que las cebras.

Glossary

Africa (**af**-ruh-kuh) the second-largest continent in the world

birth (**berth**) when a baby is born

grow (**groh**) to get bigger

miles (**mylz**) units of measuring distance, equal to 5,280 feet each

reach (**reech**) to stretch out and get something

Glosario

África El continente más grande del mundo después de Asia

alcanzar llegar a algo

crecer aumentar de tamaño

milla (la) unidad para medir la distancia, equivalente a 5,280 pies

oído (el) sentido que nos permite oír

olfato (el) sentido que nos permite oler

Resources / Recursos

Here are more books to read about the giraffes:
Otros libros que puedes leer sobre las jirafas:

Giraffes
by Emilie U. Lepthien
Children's Press (1997)

Giraffes
by John Bonnett Wexo
The Creative Company (1999)

Web sites
Due to the changing nature of Internet links, PowerKids Press
has developed an online list of Web sites related to the subject
of this book. This site is updated regularly. Please use this link to
access the list:

Sitios web
Debido a las constantes modificaciones en los sitios de Internet,
PowerKids Press ha desarrollado una guía on-line de sitios
relacionados al tema de este libro. Nuestro sitio web se
actualiza constantemente. Por favor utiliza la siguiente dirección
para consultar la lista:

http://www.buenasletraslinks.com/chl/tmb

Word count in English: 153
Número de palabras en español: 158

Index

Índice